#Dontbedumb

Be smart ... guard your heart

This Book is Dedicated to My Sweet Husband DeVone- Thank you for loving me unconditionally and speaking life over me. Thank you for encouraging me to be everything that God has created me to be. You are my gift. I am so grateful.

Contents

Introduction

This is by no means an invitation to perfection. You won't do it right every time. I didn't; I made plenty of mistakes. Instead, this is a guide for right living – an invitation to sow good seed in the direction of your destiny.

Several times a year, young women ask me to mentor them. Unfortunately, my schedule will not allow me to mentor everyone who asks. So, I decided to write a quick guide that gives a few of the life lessons I have learned along the way. I pen this guide from my heart – it's what I wish someone would have told me during my young adult years. I am so desperate to get into the lives of young adult women the wisdom to make good choices – to help them recognize that choices are seeds from which you will reap a harvest.

I always say that the place I am in my life right now is not a result of good luck; it is a result of good seed. The decisions you are making right now as a young adult woman are setting up the next 20-30 years of your life. Career, marriage, school, ministry, purpose, children ... it is all happening now ... and it is all happening so quickly.

The Bible says that there is a way that seems right to a person, but the end of that way is destruction (Proverbs 14:12). In our social media-laden society, we often compare our lives to others and make decisions based on what seems to have the most likes. It is so easy to be distracted by what every other person is doing around us, comparing our lives to someone else's Insta-story.

However, the steps to your destiny are not found looking on someone else's feed.

The truth is, only God can reveal the story that He planned for you long ago. With His truth in hand, you never have to wonder whether or not God is leading you every step of the way. The road will get windy, the path may get dark, but He will never leave you. His truth will guide your every step.

This book is divided into four sections: The Gift, The Guarantee, The Guard, and The Grace. These are four areas of truth that I believe will help guide you in these whirlwind years of young adulthood. Are these all the answers? No, not even close. But if you lean in, I believe God will open your eyes to some nuggets of truth that will change the way you think about your value, your calling, and the way you make decisions for your life.

So here is a small guide that will hopefully save you a lot of heartache and mistakes. You can definitely learn from your own mistakes, but I have heard it said that a wise woman learns from the mistakes of others. Here's to not being dumb. Here's to being women of wisdom. Be smart ... guard your heart.

The Gift

Your Purpose ... His Plans

1

You are a Gift

Let's stop for a moment and look inside our hearts. Our lives flow outwardly, and what is in our hearts eventually comes out. Our perceptions, our experiences, our fears, and our dreams are all charting the course of our lives. The Bible says in Proverbs 4:23: "Guard your heart above all else, for it determines the course of your life" (NLT). Your life is moving in the direction of what is going on inside your heart. Webster's Dictionary defines **course** as: *the act or action of moving in a path from point to point.* We are all on a course, moving from one year to another and one season to another.

Where you have arrived up until this point in your life has a lot to do with what's going on in your heart. A major part of making wise choices is recognizing who we are, why we are here, and to Whom we are called.

The Bible says that "without revelation people run wild" (Proverbs 29:18 HCSB). Without a revelation of what? The verse is speaking about people who do not have a vision for their lives or a clear perspective about what God has placed them here on the earth to do. Why do we see such destructive behaviour among our culture and our generation? It could be said that these individuals have no vision; they are just running wild.

The second part of that verse says, "but one who listens to instruction will be happy."

The New International Version of the verse states, "But blessed is the one who heeds wisdom's instructions." If we are going to live happy, blessed lives, we must listen to instruction. You need to have a clear perspective about who God is and who He has created you to be. Recognize that as you adjust your heart to the truths in Scripture and focus your attention on His great love for you, you will be setting a course for your life that is filled with happiness and blessing.

You are a gift. Just in case you were wondering, and just in case no one has ever told you: You are a gift.

Now, we all know what our own flaws are. No one has to point out to us our issues. Women are especially good at pointing out every problem we see in the mirror. It is easy for us to compare ourselves to our sisters around us. We measure ourselves by the latest trends and the latest magazine covers ... and even if we wouldn't admit it out loud, many of us believe we don't quite measure up.

But what if I told you: You are a gift to the world. You are really the only you. No seriously, God did not make anyone quite like you.

If you spend your time trying to be someone else, the world misses out on you. You are a gift to the world, and what you offer is a gift.

His Masterpiece

The Bible says that you "are God's masterpiece.

He has created us anew in Christ Jesus, so we can do the good things he planned for us long ago" (Ephesians 2:10 NLT). Think of some of the masterpieces you have seen. "The Mona Lisa," "Starry Night," the Sistine Chapel. These artists painted what was in their hearts. They poured their whole lives into creating pieces of art, and we look at them and call them masterpieces. God himself poured His heart and soul into you. He breathed His very life into you and called you "Masterpiece."

He didn't create you just to sit on a shelf and be admired by onlookers. He created you *anew* in Christ to do *"good things."* You are a gift to the world. There are "good things" that He has destined for you to complete.

I am aware that there are circumstances in our lives that taint our vision of ourselves. Abuse, abandonment, and broken relationships can skew our perspectives. But let's look at the big picture: You were His masterpiece before any of those things happened.

God's original purpose for you doesn't change based on your past experiences. When the Titanic sank off the coast of England, it contained several valuables and untold riches. It doesn't matter that the boat sank, and that the treasure may be covered in sea gunk – the treasure is still treasure. Everything the Lord intended for you remains. It doesn't matter what you've been through – the treasure remains. When we get close to God, we begin to discover all the gifts He placed inside of us. He begins to change our perspectives of ourselves, and we find out that we were truly made in His image.

One of my most prized possessions is my newest wedding ring. It was a 10-year anniversary gift from my husband that symbolizes his commitment, and his love for me. This ring is very valuable, and it is even of a higher value because it was given to me by my husband. I take care of this ring. I clean it. I watch over it, and I rarely take it off. I wouldn't dare toss it around or drag it through mud. I have never even allowed someone to try it on, because I really value it.

Maybe you have received a gift like that. Maybe it was something as simple as a new cell phone or something as precious as a grandmother's old earrings. But if it's valuable to you, you take care of it a little differently. Think about it: We protect the things we value. We protect precious gifts.

You are a gift of great value! The Creator of the Universe takes the time to call you His masterpiece. Everyone can value the beauty of a sunset or the vast expanse of a clear, blue ocean. We admire the brightness of the stars and the majesty of a snow-capped mountain range, but God did not call any of that His Masterpiece. He called YOU His masterpiece.

What if you truly saw yourself the way God sees you? He knew the world needed you, so He created you, and there isn't a single person who has ever walked the planet like you. Think about that. We know that when it comes to collectibles, the rarer the item, the more expensive it will be.

And if there is only one, it is extremely valuable. That's you – rare and extremely valuable.

Not just anyone can touch things that are valuable. If you walk into a museum, the most valued items are set behind glass or behind security fencing. These things don't beg for attention, but people are drawn to them because of their value. The way we see ourselves is the way we present ourselves to the world. Do you see yourself as worthless, confused, unworthy, or unloved? Then you do not recognize your value.

Are you begging for attention, feeling like you are changing your life in order to to meet the approval of others? Then you do not recognize your value. If we can fix the value issue, the rest will fix itself. Confidence comes when you recognize that the way God made you is masterful, and the value you carry is immeasurable.

God knows exactly how and why He made you the way that He did. He designed you specifically for the mission He has prepared for you. Let's read Ephesians 2:10 again: "You are God's masterpiece. He has created us anew in Christ Jesus, so we can do the good things he planned for us long ago."

I love that it says *long ago.* I wonder how long ago. It's amazing to think that I was in the mind of God a long time ago. He was planning my life, my family, and my mission a long time ago. God knows. He knows every step; He knows every issue. Nothing in our lives has taken God by surprise. You were created brand new in Him so that you can accomplish everything He has for you. 2 Corinthians 5:17 (NLT) states, "This means that anyone who belongs to Christ has become a new person. The old life is gone; a new life has begun!"

You are valuable because the One who created you – the One who created everything in this world – says you are! When we put our identity in anything other than Christ, we have just put our identity in something that is temporary and wavering. The Creator is the only who can call His creation what it is. Just think about it: If I walked into the Louvre and called "The Mona Lisa," "Lisa Frank," someone would probably look at me crazy. What right do I have to call that piece of art something else? I didn't create it.

In the same way, your Creator calls you Masterpiece. He calls you Blessed, He calls you Righteous, and no one (not even you yourself) has the right to call you anything different.

When you align your vision with God's vision for your life, you can't just "run wild." You begin to make choices that reflect the value God has placed on your life, and you are not likely to fall in the traps the world offers. Your calling is much more valuable than temporary pleasure. You can walk this journey out by faith, trusting God to lead you every step of the way ... because it's not your plan anyway ... it's His.

2

The Gift of Surrender

I wanted to be a doctor. Or so I thought. I love to learn. I love facts, and I knew that I was smart enough to do it. I enrolled in the first semester of Biology classes, certain that I had my life figured out. I did well memorizing the facts, learning the terminology, and memorizing the parts of the body. The problem came when I was asked to cut open a pig fetus. Um ... no. This is not for me. It also became very clear to me that I did not want to be around sick people all the time. What was I thinking? I was trying to **decide** what my destiny was, when I should have been trying to **discover** it.

I quietly disenrolled from my Biology classes and began to passionately seek the Lord. I wanted to know Him, and I wanted Him to reveal Himself to me. I had grown up in church, but I had never come to know Jesus intimately. I decided to take my relationship with God seriously. I woke up every single morning and spent time praying and reading my Bible. Some days I didn't feel anything. Some days I didn't hear anything, but I knew that if I kept praying and reading my Bible, something would happen.

Something DID happen. I fell in love. I fell completely in love with Jesus. He was it; He was my everything, and through that process of finding Him, I found myself.

This book came about because I preached a message to the young adult women in our church called, "Don't be Dumb." This was during a time when I was hearing and seeing a lot of issues arising with our young adult and teenage girls, and my heart was so grieved. The phrase, "Don't be dumb" rose up as a shout in my spirit. I wished that I could sit with each woman and talk them out of their foolish decisions.

While I was preparing the message, the Lord spoke to me and said: "Tell them they never have to guess." I pondered that for a moment, knowing that it did not come from me. It was the solid, reassuring voice of the Lord that made me smile when I heard it. I agreed. It's true. You don't have to guess. As a believer, you don't have to wander around trying out random things hoping that something will stick. You don't have to muddle around in a job that you hate for 20 years, wishing you had done something else with your life. Divine Direction is available to you! Ephesians 5:8-17 (MSG) reinforces this truth so perfectly:

"You groped your way through that murk once, but no longer. You're out in the open now. The bright light of Christ makes your way plain. So no more stumbling around. Get on with it! The good, the right, the true – these are the actions appropriate for daylight hours. **Figure out what will please Christ, and then do it.** *Don't waste your time on useless work, mere busywork, the barren pursuits of darkness. Expose these things for the sham they are. It's a scandal when people waste their lives on things they must do in the darkness where no one will see. Rip the cover off those frauds and see how attractive they look in the light of Christ.*

Wake up from your sleep,
Climb out of your coffins;
Christ will show you the light!

So watch your step. Use your head. Make the most of every chance you get. These are desperate times! **Don't live carelessly, unthinkingly. Make sure you understand what the Master wants. (Bold emphasis mine)."**

Hello! Read it again if you have to. That Scripture clearly says #dontbedumb. There is no need for you to stumble around in darkness. The light of Christ will make your path bright. Your part is to seek Him for the direction you are supposed to go in your life.

There is no way around it. If you don't spend time with the Lord, you will miss it. The end of that Scripture says that we are to make sure we understand what the Master wants. What an invitation the Lord gives us here to bypass "useless work," "barren pursuits of darkness," and "mere busywork" and dig right into the plan He has for our lives.

He admonishes us not to live "carelessly" and "unthinkingly," but I think many times, as young adults, we go into relationships, careers, and decision-making without actually thinking it through. OR we have thought it through with the wrong set of tools. If His Word has not transformed our thinking, we could be make fleshly decisions, which will lead to destruction.

Stop trying to guess what your life is supposed to be about. Fantasy worlds and fantasy relationships will lead you into a world of hurt and brokenness. We may think we know, but until we fall in love with Jesus, and until we make time and room for His Presence to influence our lives, we are only guessing. How unfortunate we are if wisdom is being offered to us and we ignore it.

We live in a world where it has become painfully easy to compare. With the flick of your thumb, you are drawn into the picture-perfect, Photoshopped realities of people all over the world. In our minds, you and I both know that life is in no way as picture perfect as people portray on social media. No one takes just one selfie before they post. Lighting, filters, angles ... bam! After 29 attempts, you post the best-looking version of yourself – #iwokeuplikethis. Although in our heads we know that social media isn't reality, we fail to guard our hearts from the notion that we don't have it all together. We see what others are doing, and we think, "Well, maybe I should do that."

But you won't find the answers for your life on someone else's page, post, or snap. You can only find your life when you lose it in Christ. Matthew 16:25 (ESV) states, "For whoever would save his life will lose it, but whoever loses his life for my sake will find it." You can only find your life in Him. Why? Because Jesus is the source of Life. He is life itself (John 14:6). Be careful that you are not looking for life outside of the source. Anything outside of this Source is counterfeit and will steal your true destiny from you.

Pray Until You Hear Him

There is nothing more fulfilling than having a living, breathing relationship with Jesus. He longs to speak to you through His Holy Spirit. Think about that ... the Creator of the Universe wants to speak to you! At first, it takes time to understand His voice. His language is different than the one we were taught as a child. He does not speak to your ears; He speaks to your spirit. There may not be anything dramatic or astounding about it. Usually, He sounds like a gentle nudge or a quiet whisper. He is speaking; we just have to tune in.

It's just like learning any other foreign language. The more time you spend in a specific country or with the people who speak that language, the easier it is for you to understand the language. I am going to learn to speak Spanish far quicker if I go to Mexico and am forced to learn the language. It's the same with God. The more time you spend with Him, the easier it is for you to understand His voice ... His language. The more time you spend in God's "country," the easier it is to discern His voice.

In high school, you most likely had to take a foreign language. One of the first things your teacher handed you is a book. You started to learn how the people speak, based on what was written down in the text. Again, it's the same with God. One of the ways you get to learn His language is by reading His Word. When you can't hear Him, read Him. It will help you to recognize when He is speaking. The pages of the Bible are full of wisdom that shows us how to live our lives. "His Word is a lamp unto our feet and a light unto our paths" (Psalm 119:105 NLT).

It's not always easy to find yourself in the Word every day, but it's always worth it. The Word of God will develop your ear to recognize His Voice. You can ask God for specific things. "Where should I attend school?" "God, what field of study do you want me to pursue?" "Lord, should I go on a missions trip? Where should I go?"

God can and will speak very specifically to you. It may not always be a voice. I have never personally heard the audible voice of God, but I have felt an impression in my spirit of what He is saying to me. In other cases, He has opened a door. On other occasions, God will answer my question through a friend. I have also read answers in the Word of God. The point is that we cannot limit God to the way He speaks, but you can always expect for Him to speak. Jeremiah 33:3 (ESV) says, "Call to me and I **WILL** answer you, and will tell you great and hidden things that you have not known." This is a promise you can stand on!

He longs to speak to you and show you the direction He has for your life. What is in your heart? Many times, we know where He is leading, but fear keeps us from going there. He has been whispering to you since you were a child the greatness that He has for you. Life has a way of trying to steal our vision and cloud our perspective. Childhood dreams can be stamped out, through the realities of our harsh world, BUT GOD! Remember, He is the author of your story, and He will equip you to do everything that He has called you to!

Don't wait until you are in a crisis before you seek the Lord and His wisdom. Cry out to God! He is waiting for you. There is no need to waste time, stumbling around in darkness. Press into the Light. Jesus is Light!

Surrender

Even after God speaks to you, you will by no means have the whole puzzle figured out. Living a life of faith means just that. You are going to need to use your faith when it comes to the plans of

God for your life. **We follow Jesus one decision at a time.** He will often give us one piece at a time, and with every obedient step, He gives us another piece. Faith is not guessing. It is obediently following what you know – trusting God for what is next. Obedience is the fruit of surrender. God will only move in your life to the degree that you surrender. He will not force you into anything. He is gentle, patient, and long-suffering, but the sooner that you surrender, the closer you are to living in the fullness of what He has for you.

Trust Him

Many of us have a hard time surrendering to God because we are still learning to trust Him. Could God really have something great for you? He does!

The Bible says:

"However, as it is written: 'What no eye has seen, what no ear has heard, and what no human mind has conceived' — the things God has prepared for those who love him— these are the things God has revealed to us by his Spirit. The Spirit searches all things, even the deep things of God"
(1 Corinthians 2:9-10 NLT).

Not only does God have good things prepared for us, He also wants to tell us what they are! The spirit of God wants to reveal those plans to us. He wants to exchange your pain and brokenness for His best, but you must surrender. What is He asking you to surrender? You know His voice. It is time. If you obey God in faith regarding whatever situation He is speaking to you about, He will meet you right there, and He will meet the need. God has so much more in store for you. You don't have to settle for the pain of the past. You don't have to settle for less than the BEST that God has for you. Surrender.

If you are having a hard time being obedient, ask yourself, "What is causing me to hesitate?" Usually it is a fear of some sort. It's usually the age-old lie that Satan has been using for ages on women. It's the lie that got Eve caught up in the garden: "God is holding out on you." We may not actually hear those words in particular, but we hear some version of them. "If you let this man go, you will not find another." "If you step out, you will fail." "God has forgotten about you." "You are not where you are supposed to be; you are a failure."

Lie after lie after lie. We will talk about lies a little later in this book, but right now, allow the love of God to shatter the lies. Remember, it may not look the way *we* think it should look, but God is working nonetheless. He is the Master Author, and He is crafting a masterpiece in your life that is greater than anything you have imagined. So just surrender.

Have you ever seen one of those painters who paints the entire painting upside down? As an observer, I'm usually like, "This looks like a mess;" "How does he even know what goes where?; "I think it's a cow."

Then the painter flips it over, and it's a picture of the Statue of Liberty. I'm always so impressed by the skill of that artist to know when and where each stroke is supposed to go. Upside down, it looks like a mess to the audience. A few in the audience may even doubt this person's artistic ability, but the painter knows what to do. He has planned every stroke and every color. Even when the painting is upside down, the artist knows where everything goes.

It's the same with God. He knows. He is the ultimate creator. The painter of sunsets, oceans, and the stars is painting your life, and even if your life feels upside down ... Surrender. Step out of the way, stop trying to figure it all out, and surrender your heart to the One who has designed something so beautiful for you. He loves you so much. He is waiting for your surrender.

If you have never given Jesus your heart, do that now. Ask Him to come into your life and be your Savior and Lord. He is a good God, and His intentions for you are only good. Ask Him to take away the pain and hurt of your past and to fill you with purpose and the gift of His Holy Spirit.

If you have accepted Jesus but you are having a hard time letting go of something in your life, repeat this simple prayer:

Jesus. I give it all to You. I surrender my plans completely to You. Do in my life what only You can do. In Your name, Amen.

3

The Gift of Preparation

Have you ever read Proverbs 31? Well, it can be a little overwhelming at first. The chapter talks about a woman who is seemingly the epitome of perfection. I mean, this woman can do it all... cook, clean, make bedspreads (you lost me right there). She is seemingly a domestic goddess, and the envy of all her neighbors.

Now, before you roll your eyes and tune this chapter out, let me share what I believe is important for you to know as a smart girl. I too, was extremely overwhelmed by this Scripture when I first read it. I mean, who is this lady? If you've never read this passage, let me give you a taste of what I'm referring to. Her life is given as an example in Scripture. Here it is (Proverbs 31:10-25 NLT):

"Who can find a virtuous and capable wife? She is more precious than rubies.

Her husband can trust her, and she will greatly enrich his life.

She brings him good, not harm, all the days of her life.

She finds wool and flax and busily spins it.

She is like a merchant's ship, bringing her food from afar.

She gets up before dawn to prepare breakfast for her household and plan the day's work for her servant girls.

She goes to inspect a field and buys it; with her earnings she plants a vineyard.

She is energetic, strong, a hard worker.

She makes sure her dealings are profitable; her lamp burns late into the night.

Her hands are busy spinning thread, her fingers twisting fiber.

She extends a helping hand to the poor and her arms to the needy.

She has no fear of winter for her household, for everyone has warm clothes.

She makes her own bedspreads. She dresses in fine linen and purple gowns.

Her husband is well known at the city gates, where he sits with other civic leaders.

She makes belted linen garments and sashes to sell to the merchants.

She is clothed with strength and dignity, and she laughs without fear of the future."

Ok, so the first few verses were already mind-blowing, but the last one always got to me. I always wondered, "Why isn't she afraid of the future?" Not only is she not afraid, she is actually laughing!

In my own life, I deal with more fear than I care to admit. For a good portion of my childhood and my adolescence, my home was unstable. My father dealt with addictions that left us poor and at times homeless. My mother did her best to keep us together. The Lord sustained us, and we never lacked for food or clothes, but for the most part, those were rough years.

I recognize that those experiences embedded a lingering fear inside of me. I never knew what the next day was going to bring, and every day, I expected more bad news. When I read this Scripture, everything in me rebelled against it. I cannot laugh without fear of the future. I am afraid of the future. This was an area in my life in which I was having a hard time trusting God.

The Holy Spirit began to speak to me about this woman as I studied further. Her actions are not about domestic skilfulness; they are about preparation. The point is that this woman is prepared! She can laugh at the future because she has prepared for the future. Go back and read it again (without the pressure of thinking that you need to turn into Martha Stewart). She is preparing. What is she preparing for? For whatever the future brings. She is making wise financial decisions. She prepares her work for each day and prepares her household for winter seasons. The point is preparation.

So how are you preparing? Whatever God brings into your life is because you have prepared for it. You want to be married? Prepare. You want a better job? Prepare. You want to carry a greater anointing? Prepare. I love my 10-year-old son. He is amazing, and I think the world of him, but I'm not going to give him my car keys. He is not prepared for that responsibility. That does not change my love for him; it actually proves my love for him. I won't give him something that he is not ready for. If we as earthly parents have the wisdom to not give our children something without their preparation, how much more our heavenly Father, who sees all and is planning out your amazing life.

Take yourself seriously

You have a calling, girl! It's a powerful, life-giving calling, and you must take it seriously. No, better yet, take yourself seriously.

I was listening to a podcast earlier this year in which the speaker said, "Take yourself seriously." For me, that brought so much clarity and light into my life. It was like she gave me permission to step into my destiny without apology. I give you that same permission. **Step into your destiny**. Pray about the things that God has for you to do and begin to prepare for them. Do you need to start or finish school? Take a missionary trip? Start your blog? Apologize to someone?

Step out!

It just takes one decision to take your life seriously.

Notice from our passage that the woman in Proverbs 31 is extremely intentional about her life. Her decisions are seemingly calculating and precise. She is careful about the field she purchases, and she is careful that her interactions are profitable. She is not idle, lazy, or stuck. She stays busy, making sure that her life is productive.

Smart girls don't sit around waiting for things to happen. They make preparation and work towards a goal. Start walking in the direction of your destiny. What small steps can you take today that will prepare you for what God has for you? It could be as simple as filling out an application or reading a book. Proverbs 16:9 states, "We should make plans – counting on God to direct us" (TLB). The Lord wants to direct your steps, but you have to take some.

Usually, the only thing that keeps you from taking those steps is fear. I made a decision in my life to deal with fear very intentionally, and I invite you to do the same. I wake up every morning and say to myself, ok – what am I afraid of today? And then I go and do that thing intentionally. We have to attack fear with the Word of God and with intentional action against that fear. Fear is a liar and our greatest enemy. It is a spirit, and it must be addressed directly.

"For God has not given us a spirit of fear and timidity, but of power, love, and self-discipline" (2 Timothy 1:7 NLT).

We attack fear with these three things:

Power- The power of God lives inside of you. The Bible says in Romans 8:11 that the same power that raised Christ from the dead lives in you. You are not powerless over your circumstances. You have resurrection power inside of you. Recognize that if God has called you to it, He has already given you the grace to do it!

Love- Hey! God loves you. He is not playing games with you, and He is not setting you up to fail. When we rest in the fact that His love is perfect, we don't have to fear the future. We all need a revelation of the perfect love of God. It is not like man's love, and it is not based on performance. It is perfect in every way. When you get a revelation of how much God loves you, fear has to leave you.

Self-discipline- This means becoming very intentional. Do the thing you fear. Joyce Meyer says, "Just do it afraid." Recognize that anytime you step out to do anything for God, fear is going to show up. Expect its arrival, and do it anyway!

You are the woman you see in your dreams, and you can do it. This generation needs you. It needs you to step into your destiny! Think about it: You were not born in 1912 or 1822. You were not born in 1536 or 70 AD. You were born in *this* generation – a generation with technological advancements beyond anything the world has ever seen. You can contact anyone in the entire world in a matter of minutes. You have access to more knowledge than the world has ever known, and God chose you to be born for such a time as this!

Think about the Bible characters of old. Do you think David thought to himself, "I am David, and they will be talking about me for years to come?" I doubt it. We know that he dealt with the same fears and struggles that all of us do, but he stepped into his destiny. He faced his fear and emerged as a voice in his generation. Acts 13:36a says, "Now when David had served God's purpose in his own generation, he fell asleep" (NIV). He served God's purpose in his generation, and God is calling you to serve God's purpose in yours!

The Guarantee

His Way... His results

4

Wisdom's Guarantee

Have you ever bought an item that has a guarantee? Usually we hear those infomercials about some item (that we cannot possibly live without) that has a money-back guarantee. We know that basically means that if it breaks or does not function properly, then we get our money back. I am always suspicious of those things. Are you telling me it might break? Is this some kind of sick reverse psychology, knowing that I would never go through the annoying process of bringing or mailing back my broken item, just to have my $9.99 back?

What in our lives is actually guaranteed? In this world, we are not guaranteed safety or comfort or that any of our plans will work. We are not even guaranteed another day. There is only one guarantee, and it is something that is sure to outlast the test of time. It is God's Word. Matthew 24:35 (ESV) states, "Heaven and earth will pass away, but my words will not pass away." His Word is our only guarantee.

Here is what I know, girls: If you do things God's way, you will get God's results. Sounds simple, doesn't it? Then why is it so difficult to do?

I think somehow we still hold on to the prideful notion that we can do things our way and still get God's results. It doesn't work. If you are not living according to the Word of God, you will not end up where you had hoped. We dealt briefly about God's Word in the previous chapter, but let's dig in a little deeper here.

Wisdom's Cry

"Wisdom shouts in the streets. She cries out in the public square. She calls to the crowds along the main street, to those who are gathered in front of the city gate:

How long you simpletons will you insist on being simpleminded?

How long will you mockers relish your mocking?

How long will you fools hate knowledge?

Come and listen to my counsel. I'll share my heart with you and make you wise" (Proverbs 1:20-23 NLT).

Can you see this scene? I picture a woman, well dressed, beautiful hair, perfectly manicured nails, highlights poppin'! She walks to the street corner and starts trying to talk to people. She politely says, "Oh sweetie, don't do that." "Oh friend, that's a poor decision." "Hello sir, it would be better if you did it this way."

NO ONE is listening. Now, this woman knows that she has the answers for all of the issues these people are facing. She has perfected the craft, she has all knowledge, she is ready to share all her secrets, and NO ONE is listening. I can see her start to get agitated, straighten her blouse, wring her hands a bit, and try to speak up a little more. "Oh hello dear, that guy is a jerk." "Oh no, sweetie, don't buy that." "I can help you with that decision."

Still, no one is listening. Her polite tone has turned into a full-blown shout. "HELLO, is anybody listening?!"

Unfortunately, no. We have all been there. We have all had a moment when we have looked back and said, "I should have listened. Wisdom was crying out to me, and I did not listen."

I remember for a season of my life (a real quick season), I got into modeling. I was taking photos and preparing myself to launch my modeling career. I had plans of stardom – "America's Next Top Model" status. I was going to hit every runway in the world. I remember sharing about an opportunity with a friend who was already in the modeling world. She simply said to me, "Remember, if they ask you for any money upfront, it is not legit." I nodded and told her that I totally understood and rushed away from the conversation with stars in my eyes.

Wouldn't you know it, the next encounter I had was with a "modeling agency" that asked me to put down $800 for my own modeling website. This site was supposed to be a place for potential clients to book me and for me to post my whole portfolio. I remember talking to the "agent" over the phone with such delight, thinking that this was the opportunity of a lifetime, and that there was no way I could pass this up.

Now, I had just been warned about this kind of thing, but I pushed that thought aside and scraped together $800. I maxed out my credit card and my mother's credit card to make it happen. Well, I guess you can figure out how well that turned out. Womp, womp, womp.

It was a hoax! Unfortunately, there was no money-back guarantee. I was stuck, and wisdom was shaking her head.

I even saw the company on "Dateline" a few years later. The owners of the company were arrested for fraud. They scammed thousands of people (including me). Wisdom is trying to talk to you, but you have to listen!

What's the source?

When we focus our lives around the Word of God, we are guaranteed God's desires for our lives. Wisdom comes from the Word of God.

My life verses are Psalms 1:1-4 (ESV). It reads:

"Blessed is the (wo)man who walks not in the counsel of the wicked, nor stands in the way of sinners, nor sits in the set of scoffers; but her delight is in the law of the Lord, and on His law (s)he meditates day and night. (S)he is like a tree planted by streams of water that yields its fruit in its season, and its leaf does not wither. In all that (s)he does, (s)he prospers."

Let's break this Scripture down:

The woman in Psalm 1 is not hanging around with sinners; she is also not hanging around those who are always talking about others (scoffers). The Bible says that bad company corrupts good character (1 Corinthians 15:33 NLT). Wait! Stop and read that again. Bad company corrupts good character. It does not say that good company influences bad people to be good. It's the other way around.

Whoever is nearest you will no doubt influence you. Be smart; guard your heart. Don't allow the opinions of your friends to take you off course. Most people are giving you advice out of their experiences, but experience is only valid if it lines up with the Word of God.

Remember, experience is only experience; it is not truth. God's Word is truth! The friends you allow in your life should be those who are willing to speak truth to you no matter what. You need friends who point you to God and remind you of His promises; not friends who try to get you to compromise in your decisions.

Do you like the life your friends have? If you do what they do, you will get what they have. Remember that you are a gift, and precious gifts must be guarded. Be careful who you allow in your circle.

The woman in Psalm 1 is guarding her circle, and she is focused on one thing. That thing has captured her heart and won her delight. It's the Word of the Lord. She meditates on the Word day and night. In this Scripture, the word "meditate" does not mean that we empty our minds and try to reach a state of "nothingness;" it means that we intentionally fill our minds. We are to intentionally fill our minds with the Word of God.

Something happens as a result of her meditation. The Scripture says that she becomes like a tree. What a powerful picture!

I think about the example of a tall Oak or a great Redwood. This woman is planted! Not flaky, not shifty, not wavering, but planted! I want to be this woman. She is solid and unmoving. Not only is she planted; she is fruitful! The older I get, the more I realize how important it is to be planted and fruitful. I have seen women jump from job to job, relationship to relationship, and church to church.

They are constantly running and never rooted. How can anyone possibly be fruitful without putting down roots? An uprooted tree doesn't produce anything, and this is what God requires of us: fruitfulness. It was His first command in Genesis.

In Genesis 1:28, God told the man and the woman to be fruitful and multiply! And even though Psalm 1 promises pretty leaves, I don't want to go through life with *just* pretty leaves. I want fruit! Fruit blesses people. Fruit transforms lives. Fruitfulness matters. Finally, the woman in Psalm 1 prospers in **everything** she does. This is the guarantee. Do it God's way...get God's results.

Be careful that **you** are not trying to determine what those results are. God is not interested in just giving you everything you want. Sometimes we don't really know what we want. God knows that if He were to give you some of your desires, they would destroy you. Along with His results is His timing. God's results are not always what we expect, but trust Him through the process. He is bringing you to a place of prosperity.

5

Guaranteed Harvest

It is often said that those things that anger you are probably pointing you to your purpose. If you have ever said, "Someone should do something about that!" That someone is probably you. I get so frustrated when I see young girls make poor decisions. I think, "Ugh...someone should have told her that's not a good decision!"

Well, this book is in response to my frustration. Am I mad at the girl? No. I am mad at the enemy! He uses the same old tricks to deceive young women over and over.

The truth is that our lives are made up of a series of decisions. If you make poor decisions, you will get poor results. You are not the exception to the rule! When we are young, we have a, "that will never happen to me" mindset. I have seen it over and over. I have seen girls jump into bad relationships, and even though wisdom tells her to get out, she remains. Play the story forward – hearts are broken and dreams are derailed. I know that every girl's story is unique and consequences are not identical, but there are always consequences when we don't do things God's way.

Seeds

Often in Scripture, the Lord likens us to farmers because we are constantly sowing, with our words and actions. Everything that we are experiencing in our lives right now can be traced back to a seed.

A seed is some decision you made from which you are now reaping a harvest. This is why spending time with the Lord and in His word is vital. There is no better way to sow seeds of success into your future than by implanting God's Word deep in your heart. Those seeds of His Word will come out in your actions and in your decision-making.

Remember, what's in your heart is charting the course of your life. You will make decisions based on the wisdom that you've tucked away in your heart, or you will make decisions based on your feelings. The Bible says that the Word of God is a two-edged sword. It separates flesh from spirit (Hebrews 4:12). It helps you to determine whether or not the situation or thought in front of you is of the Spirit or of the flesh. Without the Word implanted deep inside, you will make one lousy decision after another.

Galatians 6:7-9 (NLT) states:

"Don't be misled—you cannot mock the justice of God. You will always harvest what you plant.
Those who live only to satisfy their own sinful nature will harvest decay and death from that sinful nature. But those who live to please the Spirit will harvest everlasting life from the Spirit."

That Scripture is either good news or bad news. If you plant to please your flesh, you will reap decay and death. Listen, girls, I am pleading with you to make wise choices. You don't have to experience everything in this world. You can live a life that is set apart for God. The flesh, or your sinful nature, will never produce good things in your life. Only by sowing seeds that are pleasing to the Spirit of God will you reap a harvest of blessing.

Your flesh never wants to please God. Flesh-driven decisions will pull you away from God and from your purpose. It's not worth it. Guard your heart from people, places, words, media, and mindsets that are contrary to the Word. The enemy would love nothing more to trip you up and ruin your life. Don't give him any open door! Plant the Word in your heart, and make decisions to please the Spirit of God.

You can start sowing good seed right now! That may mean that you have to make some hard decisions. Are there relationships that are pulling you away from God? Are there habits that you are indulged in that are only gratifying to your flesh? Stop and evaluate what seeds you are sowing.

The problem with seeds is that you don't see the results right away. It may take years to see the results of a destructive decision. What if you saw the harvest of your seeds right away? What might you do differently? It's not about having good luck; it's about sowing good seed.

6
Patterns

Do you see a pattern? I did. In my family of origin, I saw a pattern that was a bit frightening to me. Pregnancy before marriage, broken marriages, poverty ... that pattern seemed to swirl around in my family line for generations. I don't know if you're familiar with the term "generational curse," but in essence, it is the **enemy's** plan for you and your family. It is the destruction that we see passed down from generation to generation. It is a spiritual condition that is modeled in the behavior of your mother and father, aunts and uncles, grandparents, and anyone else who has been in your family. Some families have generational alcoholics. Some families have generational divorce. It could be incest, homosexuality, poverty, anxiety, fear, sickness, obesity... you name it. If it has caused destruction in your family, it's a curse.

Idols
Do you want Scripture? Ok, here it is:

"You must not bow down to them or worship them, for I, the LORD your God, am a jealous God who will not tolerate your affection for any other gods. I lay the sins of the parents upon their children; the entire family is affected—even children in the third and fourth generations of those who reject me. But I lavish unfailing love for a thousand generations on those who love me and obey my commands" (Exodus 20:5-6).

God tells the Israelites that their entire family will be affected by the love that they have for other gods. Now, isn't that the truth? We must not think of the word "idol" as the tiny statues that lie in creepy, dark corners or sit on mantles (although it may be). Idols are anything that take your affection away from God. Idols are anything that you put before God.

How many stories have I heard about alcoholic parents who put alcohol before God and everything else in their world? The whole family is affected. How many stories have I heard about fathers who put a mistress before God and everything else, and the whole family is affected? I have even heard of families where "ministry" was their idol. The parents put the ministry before God and everything else, and guess what? The whole family was affected.

Here is the truth: Whatever your parents did not deal with in their generation, you will tackle in yours. Whatever you don't deal with, you will pass on to your children. Sin has consequences. It is not just about you, it's about your children, and your children's children. Again, this is either good news or bad news. In verse 5, we see a generational curse, but in verse 6, we see a generational blessing! Those who follow God's ways and deal with the sin in their own lives can pass on a generational blessing to their children.

Some of you are probably thinking, "Wait! I don't have children. How does this apply to me?"

It applies, because guarding your heart in this season is setting the stage for the next. The decisions you are making now are going to either perpetuate the curse or perpetuate the blessing.

Stop and think about it. What destructive patterns do you see in your family? Do you see any of those things playing out in your own life? Jesus died for us to have freedom in every area of our lives, but we do not step into that freedom passively. We have to actively look at the issue – **recognize it**, **repent of it**, and **choose to do something different**. You cannot do the same thing over and over and expect different results. You are not the exception to the rule.

If you do not break it, you will pass it on. We may have said, "I'll never be like..." But if we are not careful, we will end up repeating the exact same cycles that we have seen modeled for us.

It won't be easy

Anytime you are charting new territory, you are going to feel some resistance. The enemy does not like to lose territory, and he will throw heartache, distractions, disappointments, and a multitude of other challenges in your path to keep you from breaking the pattern. Guard your heart. This will not be easy, but it will be worth it.

You may feel lonely or be persecuted for the decisions that you are making. Many times, those who are closest to us are the ones who will make it the hardest, but you have to keep pressing. Remember that this is bigger than you. You are carving out a brand-new path for your family line.
 I remember talking to a girl I was mentoring right before she went to college. In the few weeks before school, she began to have nightmares every night. In addition, chaos was erupting in her home, and

she was starting to feel really discouraged. I reminded her that she was the first in her family to go to college. She was breaking a cycle, and the enemy was mad. This, of course, was not only going to affect her; it was going to affect every person that came after her. The curse of poverty was breaking in that moment. The enemy did not want to let that territory go.

Whatever curse you are breaking, recognize that you have the help of the Holy Spirit to do this. You can choose today to stop the cycle. God's Word guarantees a generational blessing on those who keep Him first in their lives. Make a decision to do it His way.

Prayer
If you recognize a generational curse in your life that you know needs to be broken, repeat this prayer out loud:

Father, I want to break every generational curse that has been attached to my family. I repent for my sin and the sins of my family. I choose to turn away from the sin of

_____ (*what needs to stop in your family. It may be several things. Confess them here*). I believe that You will help me walk out this new way of life with Your power. I believe I will see a generational blessing on my life and on the lives of my children. In Jesus's Name! Amen!

The Guard

Lies, Lust, Love

7

The Guard

Bondage. This may not be a word we think about often. The majority of us have probably never been in physical bondage. We have been fortunate to not have the chains of slavery around our ankles and wrists, and we have pretty much enjoyed a life that has been free to choose as we will. But the spiritual chains have been real. Many of us have been emotionally and mentally trapped in a habit, relationship, or situation that we would love more than anything to get out of. Sin is only pleasurable for a season.

How many of us have fallen victim to the allure of sin only to be trapped in its vicious grip? I have heard it said that sin will take you further than you wanted to go and cost you more than you wanted to pay. The enemy is ruthless. He wants nothing more than to kill, steal, and destroy your life. By the time you are in your young adult years, you have already experienced a great deal of trauma and hurt – either as a result of your own decisions or someone else's. We have all felt stuck in the regret of sin.

Strongholds

On the other hand, there is nothing quite like freedom. I remember when my life made a significant transition from the bondage and brokenness of my past to the joy of living in the freedom of Christ.

My teenage years were wrought with anguish. I was in many ways living a double life. On the outside, I wanted everyone to think that I was a perfect church girl. I pretended like I had everything together, but inside I knew that I was a complete mess. I was devastated by my parent's separation and shattered by the fact that my father left us.

I was desperately insecure, and I looked for attention from any person that would give it to me. This attention seeking caused me to lower my standards and deny everything I knew was right. I just wanted to be accepted. I was bound to fear, lust, insecurity, and failure and I carried the hurt into my young adult years. For a season, I didn't even realize that God had something better for me.

Torment is not from God. Depression is not from God. We can choose to live in our pain and shame, or we can choose to step into the light. We have all heard that God has a plan for our lives, and if you haven't, I'm telling you now: God has a plan for your life! *Jeremiah 29:11 says that the plans that He has for you are good. He has plans to prosper and not harm you, to give you a hope and a future.* Unfortunately, the enemy has plans for you too. Yes, he does. He wants nothing more than to derail God's plan for you.

I've noticed that the enemy begins when we are very little. He tries to run a theme through our lives of fear, rejection, anger, or death.

It is not uncommon for a person to experience the same type of trauma over and over in her life. He does this so that he can set up a stronghold in your life. What is a stronghold? The definition of a "stronghold" is a place that has been *fortified, so as to protect it from attack* (Oxford Dictionary).

Fortified is a strong word. It implies that this place has been packed in tight, reinforced several times, and is completely shut off. Think of every fairy tale that you have heard about the princess locked away in her castle. The idea is that she cannot get out. That castle is fortified. The enemy sets up these types of strongholds in our minds.

He lies to us about who we are and then fortifies those lies with negative experiences and more lies, and more negative experiences, until we have such a web of lies and negativity that we are sold on that idea of ourselves. His plan is for you to remain stuck behind those lies and never get out.

I like to think of a stronghold as a web of lies in our mind that is impenetrable. I don't know if you have looked a spider web lately, but spider webs are intensely intricate and very strong. Now, I have walked past a web at times and been able to swat it down easily, but those are typically one to two strand webs.

I recently asked my son to water down our porch. There were several webs there, and I didn't think they looked appealing at the front door. After 15 full minutes, with the hose at full blast, some of those webs still didn't budge. We had to physically pull them down with our hands to make the webs go away. Pulling them down was the only remedy for these fortified webs.

Second Corinthians 10:4 gives us a similar remedy for the webs in our mind. "For the weapons of our warfare are not carnal, but are mighty through God for pulling down strongholds (NKJV)." We must *pull them down* with God's mighty weapons.

Let's continue … "Casting down arguments and every high thing that exalts itself against the knowledge of God, bringing every thought into captivity to the obedience of Christ (v. 5)." We pull down these strongholds by attacking the thoughts that have built them up.

These negative thoughts are in complete contrast to the Word of God. Again, experience is not truth. God's Word is truth! If we build our lives and our beliefs based on experience, we will fall short every time. These strongholds or incorrect thinking patterns begin to affect our personality, our relationships, our confidence, and our love walk. We must recognize the web of lies that the enemy has built up in our minds and begin to tear it down.

All throughout the Word of God, the words "hearts" and "minds" are synonymous. In essence, guarding your heart means to guard your mind. What are we guarding against? We are guarding against the lies of the enemy. He shoots fiery darts into our minds to try to keep us stuck in our past and stuck in our shame. He is trying to set up his stronghold.

In my own life, I suffered from a major root of rejection. Looking back, I can see how the enemy tried to lace the theme of rejection through my life.

I didn't ever feel as if I fit in. I never quite measured up to those around me. I was taller than everyone, and I talked differently than all my peers. Add an unruly head of hair and substandard clothing, and I always felt out of place. My family innocently ridiculed my lanky body, my choice of music, and my weird appetite. I held onto those criticisms and tucked them deep into my heart. I always felt just a little different, but don't we all?

I have found that this is one of the chief lies that the enemy tries to place on us. In reality, we are NOT rejected; we are accepted. The Bible says that we have not only been accepted, but we have been adopted. Satan is rejected. He will never get to come near the throne of God again. He will never regain an entrance into heaven. He knows that his time is short and his future is doomed, so he tries to put his rejection onto us.

We can live free from this snare and every snare that the enemy lays down. Our Heavenly Father loves us and accepts us as His own. He has called us and chosen every aspect of our personalities, character, and bodies for His Glory.

Deal with It

I have seen women stuck for years with an issue that they refuse to address. It is ok to acknowledge the hurt that you experienced and recognize the real effect the incident had on you, but you don't have to carry that pain for the rest of your life.

Strongholds dictate behaviour. They will skew your perspective and limit your relationships. Strongholds will make you feel as if you have to live in poverty. Strongholds will make you feel as if you will never be enough. Strongholds will make you feel as if you won't find the right husband or have strong relationships. Identify the lie, and deal with it.

Ask yourself the hard questions. What in my life keeps tripping me up? How does this keep happening? What lie do I believe?

It begins with you. If you keep getting into bad relationships, then something is wrong with your "picker" (as I like to call it).

You only attract what you tolerate. What dysfunctions do your keep tolerating in your life? It can be a myriad of things, but only you and the Holy Spirit know what the issue is. If you are honest with yourself and with God, you can be set free. God can only heal what you reveal. He will not force His way into your heart, but if you will allow Him, His love will be the driving force to set you free.

Take the lie to God and ask Him to heal you. Seek help from a pastor, mentor, or godly counsellor. Stuffed pain only turns into bitterness and rage. As ugly as it may be, cut it open and take it to God. He wants to heal you.

I remember when I decided to seek godly counsel for my own issues. I remember how beautiful that process of healing was. I took in daily doses of God's love and began to wash my heart with the Word of God.

I remember one day waking up and realizing that I had the memories, but they didn't sting anymore. God removed the pain, and I was able to walk free.

God has so much more for you than a life of regret. Let Him heal you; let Him wash you. It may hurt to confront those things that we have tried to bury, but I promise you, freedom feels so much better than bondage.

8

Guard Down?

About 4 years into my marriage, I had a dream. It was actually two dreams in one, and they happened back to back. In the first dream, I could see myself lying in bed with my husband. At the end of my bed, I could see someone sitting at the end of our bed, dressed in a black hoodie. This person was just staring at us. I was startled and woke up.

Creepy, right? I fell back asleep and dreamt again. This time, I could see myself walking towards the back-sliding glass window and looking in the backyard. I was horrified by what I saw. I could see someone in the backyard warming himself by a fire that he had built. It was obvious that he had been living there for a long time. He had on the same black hoodie, and I knew that it was a teenage boy.

I remember feeling so violated. I experienced the same feeling that one might have if their house was broken into. I remember trying to scream through the glass window for him to get out of our backyard. I was screaming, but no sound came out. I remember the sheer terror that I felt, trying to get rid of this intruder. It was at this point in the dream that my husband rode into the backyard on a white horse, and then I woke up. Weird, right?

Attached

I thought about both of those dreams later that day and wondered what they meant. The Holy Spirit showed me that there was a third person in my marriage. He was the one sitting on the edge of my bed, and the same one warming himself by the fire in my backyard.

He was a teenage boy to whom I was attached. The backyard represented my past, and yes, he had been living there for quite some time. He was a soul tie. Maybe you have never heard the term, but it refers to a person with whom you are attached mentally and emotionally. You are connected in the spiritual realm. It can form through a sexual relationship, or through any (good or bad) agreement or vow.

Here are a few Scriptures that reference the concept of a soul tie:

"And it came to pass, when he had made an end of speaking unto Saul, that the soul of Jonathan was knit with the soul of David, and Jonathan loved him as his own soul" (1 Samuel 18:1 KJV).

"And when Shechem the son of Hamor the Hivite, prince of the country, saw her, he took her, and lay with her, and defiled her. And his soul clave unto Dinah the daughter of Jacob, and he loved the damsel, and spake kindly unto the damsel" (Genesis 34:2-3 KJV).

"Don't befriend angry people or associate with hot-tempered people, or you will learn to be like them and endanger your soul" (Proverbs 22:24 NLT).

Beautiful in its Time

For the sake of this book, I am only going to reference sexual relationships because I believe that this is a major pitfall for young women in our generation. Whenever you have sex or commit a sexual act with someone, you bind yourself to that person.

Think about that. You attach your soul to whomever you are sleeping with. In God's eyes, you are married. When God gives us a command, it is only for our protection. He knows how He created us, and He knows what is good for us. Sex before marriage creates a whirlwind of confusion and pain.

Does a soul tie always occur when you have sex with someone? Yes! In Genesis, God shows us the beautiful picture of the first marriage. He says that the man should leave his father and mother and cleave to his wife, and that the two of them will become one flesh. One flesh.

You see, in the right context, and in the safety of marriage, a soul tie can be a good thing. It binds the husband and wife together so they can become "one flesh." Outside of that union, a soul tie is detrimental. Song of Solomon 8:4 states, "Promise me, O women of Jerusalem, not to awaken love until the time is right" (NLT).

The right time is God's timing. We cannot do it our way and get God's results. We have to do it His way.

How many people might we be attached to? Unhealthy attachment is the reason we see women go back into the same abusive relationships over and over. This is why a woman can be in a current relationship and still think about relationship with an ex. This is why people cheat, marriages fall apart, and people are not satisfied in their sex lives.

I heard an illustration a long time ago that I believe bears mentioning here. Think of sex like duct tape attached to a piece of paper. Every time you sleep with someone, you attach your duct tape to his or her paper. When you break up, it rips off. Imagine that this happened over and over; duct tape to paper ... rip, duct tape to paper ... rip. What would happen after a while to that duct tape? It would lose its stickiness. Such has happened in our oversexualized society. We are bombarded with images and invitations to live sexually free, without boundaries, and without regard.

Partner after partner ... and then people wonder why they are no longer sticky when they get married. This fact is apparent in statements such as, "Sex in marriage is boring," and, "I can't imagine being with one partner for the rest of my life." The stickiness is gone.

Here is the truth: Great sex takes time. It is the result of the intimacy between two people who have taken the time to get to know each other deeply and passionately.

It's the result of committed vows being tested by the trials of life and the fight to maintain unity when you might just want to run away. Great sex happens between one man and one woman who are pledged to a life that honours God and honours each other. Any other way is a counterfeit and will leave you broken.

Guard your heart

Guard your heart against sexual sin. Nothing "just happens." Sexual sin happens as a result of a person exposing his or her heart to one compromising thing after another.

Whatever you are meditating on will manifest in your life. We discussed this fact earlier when talking about meditating on the Word of God. Meditation on His Word will bring success into your life. In the same way, if your heart is open to romance novels, steamy movies, internet porn, and explicit lyrics (to name a few things), you will manifest those things in your life. Meditation breeds manifestation.

The guard begins way before the relationship. Your heart needs tending to when you are single. If you are flooded with sexual images, ideas, and lyrics, those things will manifest in your relationships. Not only will those things manifest in your relationship, you will have oversexualized glasses on when looking for a potential relationship. You attract what you are, and if lust is in you, you will attract a lustful partner. You are so much more valuable than that!

You must know that your sexuality is also a gift that is to be preserved for only the most deserving partner. It is for the one who has committed His life to you and is ready to make a life and a home with you. No one deserves such a precious gift casually. You are a beautiful daughter of the King, and His best for you is exclusivity.

What guards have you set in your life? Each one of us is different. You and the Holy Spirit need to have a conversation about your heart and your guard. There are no set rules, but here a few things to consider as you take inventory of your lifestyle. BE HONEST.

1. Are the things you are watching on TV/movies causing you to desire sex in the wrong season?

2. Are you spending time with people who feel that sex before marriage is ok/normal?

3. Are you in a relationship right now that keeps getting too close to the edge?

4. Are you in a relationship with someone who is pressuring you for sex? (If so, RUN!)

5. Are you watching internet porn?

6. Are you reading romance novels that are stirring in you a desire for a relationship?

7. Does the music you listen to promote godly relationships or worldly ones?

8. Do you have anyone in your life who keeps you accountable in the area of purity?

If your daily choices are causing something to stir in your life before its time, you are going to have a hard time living a life of purity. You may need to make some hard choices. The choices that you will make to guard your heart in this area may not be popular, and you may have to cut off some habits. Matthew 5:30 (NLT) states, "And if your hand – even your stronger hand – causes you to sin, cut it off and throw it away. It is better for you to lose one part of your body than for your whole body to be thrown into hell."

Jesus said this, and He wasn't playing. This is a serious commitment, but serious commitment is what it is going to take to guard your heart. Our culture is fighting for your purity. You are going to have to fight back!

Detach

If you have struggled in this area of sexual purity, take a moment and ask God to put those desires back to sleep. He will do it! He will restore those areas that are broken and shameful, but we must be honest and give it to Him. If you are attached to someone or someones in your past, God can set you free from them as well.

Remember at the end of my dream, I mentioned that my husband rode in on a white horse? Well, I knew that meant God was telling me that there were some things I needed to tell him about my past. So, I did. I told my husband, and he prayed for me.

He prayed that God would loose me from those old relationships. He prayed that God would sever those ties and set me free from anyone to whom my soul was attached. You know what? I was set free! I don't know how to describe it, except to say that I felt like a breath of fresh air filled my lungs.

Two things are important to note here: I told someone, and I prayed. James 5:16 (NLT) states, "Confess your sins to each other and pray for each other so that you may be healed. The earnest prayer of a righteous person has great power and produces wonderful results." If you are involved in a compromising relationship, tell a godly friend and ask for accountability. Have her pray with you and help you to cut off unhealthy ties. Adding a godly friend to your life is a great way to maintain your guard.

If you need to detach from someone, you can pray that same prayer that my husband prayed over me. Don't rush through it. Spend some quiet time with God revisiting those painful relationships. Ask Him to cut the ties. Ask Him to put the love back to sleep and ask Him to set you free!

9

That's not your Husband

It's been a few years since the term "thirsty" made its debut on the pop culture scene. If you are not familiar with this term, it was a way to describe a woman who seems really desperate for attention and relationships. This woman dresses and behaves in a way that lets everyone know that she is to be desired and that she wants something from a man. She is desperate, seeking, wanting, but never satisfied.

Now, the term is new, but the concept made its debut when Jesus walked the earth. John 4 tells us that Jesus met a woman who was "thirsty." In actuality, she may have been physically thirsty because the location of their meeting was a water well. Jesus, going about His daily tasks and ministry, purposed to meet a thirsty woman at a well. Jesus broke through barriers of culture, ethnicity, and convenience to meet this woman, but the Bible says that he "had" to go there. Jesus rearranged his journey to get to this woman. He made her a priority. He knew that something special was going to happen as a result of this encounter. He knew that her thirst ran deeper than a well. Her thirst could not be quenched by physical water alone. She needed living water. I encourage you to read the entire account in John 4, but for the sake of this chapter, let's pick up in verse 9:

"The Samaritan woman said to him, 'You are a Jew and I am a Samaritan woman. How can you ask me for a drink?' (For Jews do not associate with Samaritans.) Jesus answered her, 'If you knew the gift of God and who it is that asks you for

a drink, you would have asked him and he would have given you living water.'

*'Sir,' the woman said, 'you have nothing to draw with and the well is deep. Where can you get this living water? Are you greater than our father Jacob, who gave us the well and drank from it himself, as did also his sons and his livestock? Jesus answered, 'Everyone who drinks this water will be thirsty again, but whoever drinks the water I give them will never thirst. Indeed, the water I give them will become in them a spring of water welling up to eternal life.' The woman said to him, 'Sir, give me this water so that I won't get thirsty and have to keep coming here to draw water.' He told her, 'Go, call your husband and come back.' 'I have no husband,' she replied. Jesus said to her, 'You are right when you say you have no husband. The fact is, you have had five husbands, and the man you now have is **not your husband.** What you have just said is quite true.'*

Not your Husband

Ouch! That was a sting. I can only imagine the look on this woman's face as Jesus confronted plainly what she fought hard to conceal. Cultural history tells us that women in this day did not typically go to water wells alone; they went as a group of gals. They sat around the wells and talked and gossiped and caught up on each other's lives. But this woman was alone.

She was most likely a social outcast: the girl with a reputation. We can see from this narrative that she had suffered failed relationship after failed relationship, and now the person she was with was "not her husband." We don't know the details of her past, but somehow she had come to the point, where any old relationship would do. She was thirsty – thirsty for love, attention, and affection. She longed to be full, and her drug of choice was men.

I see this many times in young women, who also long to be full. So many of us have made the mistake of thinking that a man would fulfill all of our needs. It may be that your earthly father was absent or failed to give you the affirmation that as a little girl you so desperately needed. Now as an adult, when insecurity drives your need for a relationship, you are headed for brokenness and disaster. Just like the woman at the well, you will settle for a counterfeit when God has so much more!

The Source

Let's settle the first issue. You can never receive from a man what you can only receive from God. Relationships are beautiful, and they are from God. Marriage is beautiful, and it is from God, but people are just resources; they are not the Source. If you put a constant demand on a resource, and not the Source, you will both be left dry.

People cannot give you what only God can give you – affirmation, security, purpose and unconditional love. He is the Source.

You cannot put all the burden of your emotional and affirmation needs on a person. They are not designed to fulfill that need. This is why marriages fail and people are left wanting.

Before you even think about getting into a marriage or dating relationship, you must know who you are in Christ. When you are receiving that constant flow of living water from your relationship with Jesus, you will easily weed out the counterfeits. You may have heard this before, but it is worth repeating. Two halves do not make a strong relationship; two whole people do, and wholeness is only found in the Presence of God!

Jesus invited the woman at the well into a relationship that would give her an overflow of life. Her response was typical. *Yes, of course, give me the water that never runs dry. I don't want to have to keep coming back to this well over and over.* But before he could take her forward, he had to confront her issue. He peeled back the layers of her heart, and said to her, "Go call your husband."

I can imagine that the task of drawing water was arduous. The water pots in the ancient world were huge and probably difficult to carry. She was looking for Jesus to give her a quick fix to her water problem. I assume that she did relationships the same way.

If this one doesn't work, I'll get the next. If that one doesn't work, I'll try the next. Well, marriage doesn't work, so I won't do that again.

I'll just live with the guy. Jesus didn't want to give her quick fixes; He wanted to give her life.

You have to check your heart and your motives before you walk into a dating/marriage relationship. Allow the Holy Spirit to peel back the layers of your heart and ask yourself some hard questions. What is driving you? Is it fear? Is it insecurity? Is it pride? Is it impatience? One of my favorite Scriptures is Proverbs 27:7 (TLB): "Even honey seems tasteless to a man who is full; but if he is hungry, he'll eat anything!"

Did you see it? Can I have a little bit of creative license with the Bible and for the sake of this chapter change the word "hungry" to "thirsty," and "eat" to "drink?"

SO, here is my version:

Even water seems tasteless to a woman who is full, but if she is thirsty, she'll drink anything!

A thirsty girl will drink anything. We have all seen relationships that seem a little off. Why is she with him? Why won't she leave the abusive relationship? Why is she settling for someone who she doesn't really want? It's because thirsty girls drink anything.

Fill Up

Your singleness is one of the most precious times in your life. You have nothing better to do than to fill up on living water.

Spend as much time with the Lord as possible. Pursue His call for your life. In your singleness, God is the only one to whom you answer. Allow Him to love on you and fill you with the affirmation and unconditional love that your heart desires.

Allow the living waters of His Presence to fill you up and flow out of you. When you are full, then you are no longer looking for someone to complete you. Actually, when you are full, you are not looking at all.

The man who finds you will find you in Christ, and side-by-side, you will accomplish great things for the Kingdom of God. Your love story will be a testimony for your children and future generations.

Sign and Wonders

On another note, I feel I should lay down some practical considerations when deciding on a dating relationship. I got married very young, and missed much of the dating scene. But I have noticed that there are some weird things out there – stuff that you should be aware of. I like to call it signs and wonders (I actually stole the name from my Uncle Jerry). Over years of mentoring and counseling young women, I have compiled a list of some signs that should raise red flags for you:

1. If he doesn't have any friends or accountability, that is a sign, and you need to wonder about that.

2. If he is disrespectful to his mother, that is a sign, and you need to wonder about that.

3. If he seems controlling, that is a sign, and you need to wonder about that.

4. If he has no direction for his life, that is a sign, and you need to wonder about that.

5. If he cannot keep a job, that is a sign, and you need to wonder about that.

6. If he can't stick to a commitment (ministry, appointments, school, etc.) that is a sign, and you need to wonder about that.

7. If he is not interested in volunteering or getting involved at a church, that is a sign, and you need to wonder about that.

8. If he is involved in *all* the ministries at church, that is a sign, and you need to wonder about that.

9. If he needs to know where you are at all times, that is a sign, and you need to wonder about that.

10. If he says, 'God told him' that you are his wife, that is a sign, and you need to wonder about that. (Actually, my husband told me this... and I did wonder about it for a while, but it turned out to be true. LOL)

11. If he is broke, that is a sign, and you need to wonder about that.

12. If he is not thinking about marriage, that is a sign, and you need to wonder about that.

13. If he doesn't know God, don't wonder; just run!!

You have to be brave enough to say, "That's not my husband." You have to be so satisfied with the sweetness of Jesus that you are not choosing relationships in desperation. If marriage is not the end game in your dating relationship, what is the point? There should be a purpose to everything that you are doing, especially relationships. Be patient, beautiful one: God is preparing the right one for you.

There is no need to waste your time on purposeless relationships. If you are in a relationship that you know is not from God, be brave enough to say, "That's not my husband," and get out of it. The longer you hold onto what's not for you, the longer it takes to get to the one who is for you. (Side note: God will NEVER tell you that someone else's husband is yours. If you are having that thought, you need to go back to the beginning of this chapter and start reading again.)

What is for you is for you! You don't need to compare or covet what someone else has.

Let God Write your Love Story

After her life-changing experience with Jesus, the woman at the well led many to Jesus. His words, compassion, and honesty so pierced her soul and transformed her heart that she became a powerful witness for Him. We do not know if she ever came into another marriage or dating relationship, but we do know that she walked away from that well full.

She was full of so much life that she could not keep it to herself. She told her town to come and hear a man "who told me everything I ever did (John 4:39)." See, she was no longer ashamed of her story. In fact, by the end of that day, she had a new story, with a different man. When God writes your story, there is no shame. You will never regret doing things God's way. God wants nothing more than to give you the desires of your heart, but until then, guard it against counterfeits and flakes. Allow God's living water to fill you to overflowing. He will never leave you wanting.

The Grace
Repentance and the Race

10

The Grace for our Mistakes

In my early 20s, I started to recognize very quickly that I was heading in the wrong direction. I wanted my life to matter, and I knew that the choices I was making were leading me into a life of destruction. I was weary from a difficult upbringing, saddened by the loss of my relationship with my father, and confused about the direction in which I was going. I knew I was making choices out of my pain, and I knew it was time for me to repent.

"Repent" is an interesting word. It is often used in churches when people are asked to give their lives to Jesus. It is used in the context of encouraging people to apologize to God for the things that they have done, and for them to accept His free gift of salvation. However, in the original language, repent has a slightly different meaning. In the Greek, the word is "meta-noia," which means to change your mind. It doesn't mean beg for forgiveness or cry on your knees in agony. It literally means to change your mind.

When we truly repent, we change our minds about the things that we were doing, and we don't do them anymore.

True repentance is seen in your future choices, not in one moment of regret. If you have been making destructive decisions, it is time to repent, and you know what? It's as easy as changing your mind.

Change Your Mind

Change your mind about that relationship. Change your mind about that addiction. Change your mind about the friends that are in your circle. Change your mind about your past. Change your mind about your future. Change your mind about yourself (Remember: you are a gift).

You are not in too deep. Do not allow the enemy to make you feel as if you cannot get out of whatever hole you have been in. If we allow him, the enemy will tell us that we have wasted too much time, or that it's all over. He will make you feel as if God's plans for you are over, and that you will never be used by God. But those are all lies. Remember, that is the enemy's plight, not yours. It is all over for him, but not for you!

You may not be able to change what is going on around you, but you can change your mind. This is usually the first step to getting out of a mess.

I remember reading a quote that said, "You are not a tree; you can move." Now I know that is silly, but for me in that season, it was profound. I thought to myself, "Yeah, I'm not a tree; I can move." And so can you. Get up and go in the other direction. It is not too late.

God will change you

You can never earn the love of God. He loved you when you were a sinner, and there is nothing that you can do that will separate you from His love. It is prideful to think that our sin is greater than His love.

His love conquers every sin, every mistake, and every fear. Do not ever think that your mistakes can keep you from receiving all that God has for you. When we repent, the Bible says that He is faithful and just to forgive us and to cleanse us from all unrighteousness (1 John 1:9). This Scripture shows us that He is committed to us, and He will cleanse us. He loves us in our mess, but He will never leave us in a mess.

His grace is what empowers us to live a holy life and to lay down our lives for Him. As I surrendered my heart to the leading of the Holy Spirit and the Presence of God, He began to illuminate the dark places in my soul and transform my broken heart. Repentance is not a one-time task; it happens over and over as we allow God to transform the way we think.

Through this process of transformation, you will see how God can turn our mistakes for our good and for His glory. There are two ways that the Bible says we overcome: The Blood of the Lamb, and the word of our testimony (Revelation 12:11 NLT). That pain that you experienced, those mistakes that you made ... use those stories to tell the world of the goodness of God.

Use your story to show others how He rescued you from a life of darkness. Use that relationship drama to teach another girl about the "signs and wonders" I shared about earlier. Use your frustrations to tell another girl, "#dontbedumb." God never wastes our pain, and you shouldn't either. He will use every part of your life for His glory if you allow Him.

11

The Grace to Endure

Your life is made up of seasons – some good, some bad, some fruitful, and some seemingly barren. Even when we have made wise choices, there will be seasons when we are waiting for the harvest of seeds we have planted. You almost never sow and reap in the same season, and in order to live well, you will need to learn endurance.

Endurance is not a fun word. I don't know what images the word "endurance" conjures up for you, but for me, it's images of running. I like to run ... sort of. I mean, I tolerate it. I like the way that I feel afterward, but the process is always so rigorous. I always start out really strong, but about halfway through my run, everything in me wants to quit. My legs start hurting, my lungs start telling me I'm going to pass out, and my brain is questioning why I am putting myself through such unnecessary torture.

The Bible compares our spiritual life to a race. Hebrews 10:36 states, "Patient endurance is what you need now, so that you will continue to do God's will. Then you will receive all that he has promised" (NLT). It is really not about how you start the race; the prize is for the ones who finish.

My heart breaks when I see young women start off on this race strong, and then end up back in the same mess God delivered them from. Why does that happen? Because emotions cannot sustain you on this walk of faith.

We do not walk by emotions; we walk by faith, and there will be some seasons that are really dark. There will be some seasons when God seems silent, and if your relationship with God is based on your feelings, you will falter.

I went through a 4-year period in my young adult years when I felt like everything was falling apart. I was married, I had 2 children, and I was miserable. I knew that God had called me and that the plan He had for my life was secure, but nothing in my life looked like what He promised. I suffered the loss of relationships, a baby, my home, and a few prized possessions. I was so confused during that time, and I kept wondering, "God, when will this all change?"

But it was during that season that I learned to trust God. I knew He was with me. I did not understand Him, but I trusted Him, and when the road seemed darkest, I knew that He was still the light leading me and guiding me. I learned to press past my quit and keep my eyes focused on Him. In the midst of that dark season, He refined my calling and sharpened my spiritual ears. He taught me to run with endurance.

See, if my relationship with God were based on my feelings, I would have given up right then. As soon as He stopped (seemingly) speaking, I would have lost heart. But I knew enough about God and His Word to know that even though I was walking through a valley of the shadow of death, He was with me (Psalm 23). I did not need to feel Him ... my faith went deeper than my feelings.

Don't Quit

As you follow Jesus, there will be seasons when you will ask yourself, "Where am I, and God, what are You doing in my life?" I've been there many times. There have been dark, dark seasons where I felt as if I was doing everything right, but everything was going wrong.

God was strengthening my endurance in those times. Faith has to be tested, and trust in God deepened. It has been through some of my darkest seasons that I found out things about God that I would have never known if things were perfect.

You will need to press past **YOUR** quit. Yes, you will want to give up. Right choices are not popular, and living a life of complete surrender to Jesus may not be met with applause, but keep running. Maybe you have been serving the Lord for a long time, and it seems like His promises are slow in coming. Just keep running. You are learning endurance. Allow this process that you are in to deepen you, and make your faith stronger. Don't waste a season. Every season is preparation for the next. Steward the pain and the frustrations of one season so that you will be stronger in the next season.

There is a story in the Bible about a group of people who missed their season. The children of Israel were the people that God chose out of all the people on the earth. In the book of Numbers, the Bible shows us that there were promises and blessings in store for them, but they could not receive their promise because of unbelief.

These were the people who saw God part the Red Sea. These were the people who were fed straight from heaven. Yet, they were unbelievers. That is astounding to me. Complaints replaced their praise; fear conquered their belief, and they were left wandering in a wilderness for 40 years.

I have seen some wanderers in our day. Yes! Modern-day Israelites, who know of God, but don't know God – who are walking around in wildernesses of fear, doubt, insecurity, and unbelief. These are people who do not believe that the God of the Universe is in control and knows what He is doing in their lives.

Whatever you are going through in this season, do not allow complaints to take the place of your praise. Do not allow fear to conquer your belief. Guard your heart against the urge to quit.

Don't Rush

There was not a person in the Bible who did not endure a process on the way to their destiny. God is more concerned about what is going on inside of you than what is going on around you. Do not rush a season. James 1:3-4 states, "For you know that when your faith is tested, your endurance has a chance to grow. So let it grow, for when your endurance is fully developed, you will be perfect and complete, needing nothing" (NLT). Endurance needs a chance to grow.

It would be so amazing if things grew quickly. That is how we want things to happen in our lives. We like fast: fast food, lightening internet speed, and our chats in a snap! But anything that stands the test of time needs a chance to grow.

We don't want "fad faith;" we want full-grown faith and endurance. Give yourself the grace to grow.

A good thing in the wrong season is a bad thing. For example, oranges taste better in the winter, and watermelon in the summer. The Bible says He makes all things beautiful at the appointed time (Ecclesiastes 3:11). Rushing will cause us to chase a good thing in the wrong season. Wait on the Lord. He knows the path that He has for you to take; trust His timing and leading.

Comparison

You cannot run your race looking at someone else's. The race that God has for you is for you alone. One sure way to trip yourself up and cause you to slow down is by comparing your race to someone else's. Comparison kills. Yes, I know that was a strong statement, but it's true. Comparison will kill your future, it will kill your dreams, and it will kill your focus.

You have to know *your* season. Are you in a season of waiting? Are you in a season of growth? What is God doing in you right now? If you do not recognize the season you are in, you will be tempted to compare your race with the girl next to you. There are beautiful things that the Lord is doing in you in this season, but you will miss them if you are stuck in comparison.

If you try to make decisions in your life based on what is happening in someone else's life, you run the risk of making some decisions that will cause you regret. People are not the standard by which you measure your life. Jesus is the standard.

Hebrews 12:1-2a beautifully depicts this truth: "Therefore, since we are surrounded by such a huge crowd of witnesses to the life of faith, let us strip off every weight that slows us down, especially the sin that so easily trips us up. And let us run with endurance the race God has set before us. We do this by keeping our eyes on Jesus, the champion who initiates and perfects our faith" (NLT).

We can only keep running when our eyes are on Jesus, not on those around you. He is the champion of our faith.

Here are a few things that I have learned about seasons:

1. God will rarely change your season when you are just exhausted and ready to quit. You have to press past your quit.

2. You cannot live in every season the same way. Each season will require something different from you (i.e. If you are in school, you cannot hang out with friends as often. If you are a new wife, you will have to prioritize time with your husband). Recognize what season you are in and adjust accordingly.

3. When you cannot hear God, read God. He writes the way He speaks. He speaks the way He writes. If He seems silent or distant, stay committed to the Word of God. Seasons change, but His Word remains the same.

4. You are not your feelings. Let me say that again. **You are not your feelings.** You cannot trust your feelings because they will change from day to day. Keep running.

5. There will be times when you know where you are going, but you don't know where you are. Don't give in to a spirit of confusion. Keep running.

6. God will never tell you to leave an assignment because you are frustrated or offended (i.e. leaving you church because you are mad at someone). You need to work through that frustration and/or offense before you move on.

7. Transition is hard. It is always hard, and someone is usually hurt in the process. You cannot stop transition from happening. Go with the flow.

8. Change is a part of life. Embrace the new things that God is doing. God loves doing new things.

9. If you are not growing, you are dying. There is no such thing as stagnant.

10. Guard your heart against a spirit of disappointment. Keep dreaming. Keep hoping. Keep believing.

There are so many promises in the Word of God, and this one is one of the best: "So let's not get tired of doing what is good. At the right time we will reap a harvest of blessing if we don't give up" (Galatians 6:9 NLT). You can do this, girl! You can live a life of holiness and make wise choices. We are writing the story for future generations. Our daughters and our daughter's daughters are counting on us.

If you've stopped running, get back up. Your race is still set before you, and the whole host of heaven is cheering you on! Jesus is your champion, and He is cheering you on, and so am I. When you and I are nearing the end of our lives, we will look back and say that we ran well, and we ran without regret. We will pass the torch to future generations – a baton that reads: Be smart … guard your heart.

My Prayer for You

I pray that you walk in wisdom and follow God's call on your life. I pray that you walk in the fullness of God's will, and that you know and recognize the great love that God has for you. I pray that you walk out of your shame, walk out of your past, and start to live in the light of His grace. I pray that you dream again, hope again, and trust that God's plan for you is bigger than you'd ever imagine. I pray that your relationships are fruitful, and that God gives you the desires of your heart. I pray that you demolish every curse over your life and chart a new path for your family. I pray that you would recognize who you are and live a life of adventure and beauty.

The world is waiting for you. Go get 'em, smart girl!

I Am Who God Says I am

(Use these Scriptures to start tearing down strongholds)

I am a new creation

"Therefore, if anyone is in Christ, he is a new creation. The old has passed away; behold, the new has come." (2 Corinthians 5:17 ESV)

I am chosen, I am royal, I am His

"But you are not like that, for you are a chosen people. You are royal priests, a holy nation, God's very own possession. As a result, you can show others the goodness of God, for he called you out of the darkness into his wonderful light." (1 Peter 2:9 NLT)

I am His masterpiece

"For we are God's masterpiece. He has created us anew in Christ Jesus, so we can do the good things he planned for us long ago." (Ephesians 2:10 NLT)

I am the temple of the Holy Spirit

"Don't you realize that your body is the temple of the Holy Spirit, who lives in you and was given to you by God? You do not belong to yourself." (1 Corinthians 6:19a NLT)

I am His friend

"No longer do I call you servants, for the servant does not know what his master is doing;

but I have called you friends, for all that I have heard from my Father I have made known to you." John 15:15 ESV)

Greater is He that is in Me

"But you belong to God, my dear children. You have already won a victory over those people, because the Spirit who lives in you is greater than the spirit who lives in the world." (1 John 4:4 NLT)

I can do all things through Christ

"I can do all things through him who strengthens me." (Philippians 4:13 ESV)

I am Chosen

"You did not choose me, but I chose you and appointed you that you should go and bear fruit and that your fruit should abide, so that whatever you ask the Father in my name, he may give it to you." (John 15:16 ESV)

I am fearfully and wonderfully made

I praise you, for I am fearfully and wonderfully made. Wonderful are your works; my soul knows it very well. (Psalm 139:14 ESV)

I am more than a conqueror

"No, in all these things we are more than conquerors through him who loved us." (Romans 8:37 ESV)

I am triumphant

"But thanks be to God, who in Christ always leads us in triumphal procession, and through us spreads the fragrance of the knowledge of him everywhere." (2 Corinthians 2:14 ESV)

Thejoycompany.info

Made in the USA
San Bernardino, CA
23 March 2018